Threads of Deceit

Margaret McAllister

Illustrated by Tim Clarey

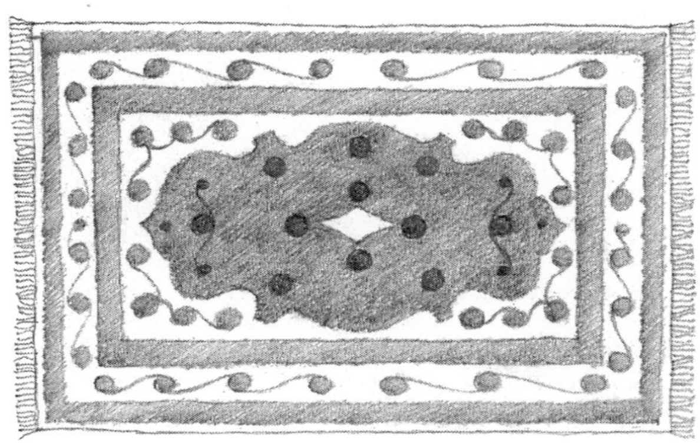

PACIFIC LEARNING

Illustrated by **Tim Clarey**
Photography: p. 4 Earl Kowall/Corbis UK Ltd.; pp. 4–5 Corel; p. 5 B. Turner/Trip & Art Directors Photo Library; p. 14 J. Hurst/Trip & Art Directors Photo Library; p. 23 Simon Arnold/Eye Ubiquitous; p. 38 Denis Cameron/Rex Features; p. 92 James Davis Worldwide; pp. 92–93 Corel; p. 93 John Stanmeyer/VII; p. 94 Manish Swarup/Associated Press; pp. 94–95 Corel; p. 95 Dennis Cameron/Rex Features
U.S. edit by **Alison Auch**

This Americanized Edition of *Threads of Deceit,* originally published in England in 2003, is published by arrangement with Oxford University Press.

13 12 11 10
10 9 8 7 6 5 4 3 2

Published by
Pacific Learning
P.O. Box 2723
Huntington Beach, CA 92647-0723
www.pacificlearning.com

ISBN: 978-1-59055-448-7
PL-7614

Printed in The United States

Contents

Introduction

Imagine... A small child wakes up and thinks of the new day ahead of him: no annoying parent to tell him to get up, no school, no books to lug. Does it sound like fun? It isn't. The reality for this child is another hard day of exhausting work with no pay, horrific surroundings, very little food, no time off to talk or to play with friends, and finally, after a beating, a brief nap on the floor of a dirty room. Why? Because this young boy is a slave, sold to a factory owner who hides him from the child inspectors or bribes them to turn a blind eye to his desperate situation.

How it can be done...
Adult rug weavers work in open, airy conditions

Thankfully, some – the lucky ones – are found and rescued by dedicated people working to free children from slavery.

How it should never be done... The faces of these rescued child laborers say it all. Notice how incredibly young these children are. Most of you had just started school at this age.

CHAPTER

Earth and Dreams

The brick-red earth was hot and hard under Sanjit's bare feet. When he looked up, he had to squint his eyes against the blinding sun.

Far away in the distance, something flashed. It might be sunlight on a car windshield. In towns and cities, there were the vans, trucks, and towering buildings that Sanjit rarely saw. Somewhere like that, his older brother was working now. That left eleven-year-old Sanjit as the oldest child still at home.

That would change soon, though! He wanted to be out in a big, noisy city doing something important, something to make his parents proud of him. Above all, he wanted to earn money and help his family. Yet he was still here, plowing this little patch of land where they grew just enough to feed themselves and have a little – a very little – to sell at the market.

Sanjit's mother made flower garlands. Yet there were never quite enough garlands, so there was never quite enough money, never quite enough food, for all of them. Sanjit had three sisters and a brother so tiny he could hardly walk without tumbling over.

Everyone said Sanjit was good at plowing, but that was nothing. He wasn't as good as Bikas, his big brother. He wanted to excel at something Bikas couldn't do.

One day, if he earned enough money, Sanjit would learn to read and write. You could get better work and earn more money if you could read and write. Yet that idea was absurd. You needed money to go to school in the first place. Even by saving every single rupee they could, his parents would never have enough money to send even one of their children to school.

"Sanjit!"

He jumped. It was his sister's voice. She was shouting something from the next field, but he couldn't hear more than a few of her words – something about "Mom" and "house." He narrowed his eyes, shook his head at her, and turned the plow neatly at the end of the furrow. If plowing was all he was good for, at least he'd establish that he was the best. Soon, he was close enough to hear what Mala was saying as she hopped and fidgeted with impatience.

"Mom says to come home right now," she said. "She says to wash up and come in looking spotless, because we have a visitor."

If he asked who it was, she wouldn't tell, so he didn't ask.

"Don't you want to know who the visitor is?" she asked, exasperated.

He shrugged. Mala gave up and flashed bright white teeth in a smile.

"Uncle Vikram!" she said, darting away. Sanjit followed her without attempting to keep up. He was growing into the adult world and she wasn't. She still got excited by a visit from Uncle Vikram. Sanjit used to be like that. When he was younger, Uncle Vikram had been his hero.

When Sanjit was little, he hadn't understood the way his mother looked at Uncle Vikram. She never smiled much when he was there, and she said little, as if she wanted him to go as soon as possible. Uncle Vikram was fun. He would tickle the children and tease them until he got bored and seemed to forget they were there. He was handsome and entertaining, and he knew about life in the cities. Yet as he grew up, Sanjit felt less sure about Uncle Vikram.

"Vikram only comes here when he wants something," his mother had once said. Sanjit knew he wasn't supposed to hear that.

Soon, he was sitting on the ground outside the house while Uncle Vikram admired how much he had grown and asked him about the

plowing. His mother sat with them, making garlands with quick, deft fingers. She glanced up at Uncle Vikram now and then, saying nothing. His father was there too, and it was unusual for his father to stop work in the middle of the morning. Then, calmly and carefully, Uncle Vikram opened the door to Sanjit's dreams.

CHAPTER

Uncle Vikram

"Now, Sanjit," said Uncle Vikram, "we've been talking about you. Isn't it time you saw something more than this little patch of land? Do you want to be a man of the world?"

It was too sudden, and Sanjit was taken aback. It was as if Uncle Vikram could see into his mind, because of course he wanted to see the world. Uncle Vikram couldn't be talking about now, though. Perhaps he meant the future – years away.

"Answer your uncle, Sanjit," said his father.

"I, I don't know," stammered Sanjit. It made him feel stupid, but he truly didn't know. He glanced at his parents, but their faces told him nothing.

"What do you mean?" he asked.

"I know of a craftsman in the city who needs boys to train," said Uncle Vikram. "You can learn a trade, Sanjit, and be your own master one day."

"If you please, what trade?" asked Sanjit.

"Your uncle can find you work in a carpet factory," said his father. His mother looked up as if she were about to say something, but Uncle Vikram was too quick for her.

"World-famous carpets," he cried. "Think of it, Sanjit!"

Sanjit's home didn't have carpets, but he had seen them in the market and admired them. They were usually rich with deep, jewel-like colors, and he could only imagine

Women selling rugs in a street market like the one Sanjit has seen

what it would be like to walk from room to room with the lush feel of carpet under his feet. Carpets were too good to walk on, though. They should be hung on walls and admired. They had elaborate patterns woven into them, row upon row.

"Would I learn to make those patterns?" he said. "Those carpet patterns?"

"I'm sure you would, if you turned out to be good at it," said Uncle Vikram. "Look at those hands!"

Sanjit looked at his hands. His fingers were long and slender. Sometimes he helped his mother with the garlands, and she said he had agile fingers.

"Those hands are wasted here," declared Uncle Vikram.

"Every boy should learn to grow food," said Sanjit's father firmly. "You can't eat carpets, after all. He can use a plow, and that's a great help to the family."

"He needs more than that," said Uncle Vikram, with a smile so radiant that Sanjit couldn't help smiling back. "He needs skills. He needs education."

Sanjit's mother looked up sharply. It was as if she felt the flash of hope in Sanjit.

"Education?" she asked.

"It's part of the deal," said Uncle Vikram. "At the carpet factory he will learn to read and write. Didn't I mention that? Maybe he will learn math too. Who knows what else? He has a lot of potential."

After that, it was soon settled. When Uncle Vikram mentioned the money that must be paid to the factory owner to employ him, Sanjit felt as if a cloud had covered the sun. His parents' faces grew shadowed too.

"Don't worry," said Uncle Vikram. "If you can't afford it, they'll just take it out of his wages until it's paid."

"I need to earn money for the family, though," said Sanjit.

"You will." Uncle Vikram smiled again. "You will. Think of it, Sanjit!"

Sanjit did think of it, all the time, as he waited for the day when he would go to the carpet factory. Every day of plowing and weeding was long and tedious, until his last day at home. That day, it seemed to take forever until the sun lowered and it was time to go back to the house and eat.

Sitting on the floor with his bowl in front of him, eating the rice and **dhal** that tasted the way only his mother could make it, he thought of the long journey ahead. He had no idea of where he would be by this time tomorrow, or what he would eat, or where he would sleep. Nobody had told him when he could return home to see his family, or whether they might come to see him. He ate the dhal slowly, wishing there could be more.

Too agitated to sleep, Sanjit was up early and ready to go long before Uncle Vikram arrived to walk with him to the small town. He was glad nobody else was there to see him giving his mother one last, hard hug, pressing his face against her old **sari**.

"When I learn to write, I'll send you letters," Sanjit said. "One day, I'll make you a carpet. One with red in it." It was his mother's favorite color.

"Every single day and night, I'll keep the picture of your face in my heart," she said. She wrapped up some **chapatis** in a cloth and pushed them into the pocket of his shorts. "You'll need to eat that on the way."

It was time to go. All the way to the town, Sanjit kept his head up and looked straight ahead so Uncle Vikram would not see his sorrow and his tears.

CHAPTER

Long Day's Journey

Sanjit was feeling better by the time they were standing outside a row of offices near the edge of town. This was the beginning of his incredible adventure, and he tried not to be disappointed that the place was so drab and dilapidated. It all looked a lot better when

Uncle Vikram pointed to a van. A van! It was filthy white, rusty, and dented, but that wasn't the point.

"Do you see that?" said Uncle Vikram. "You're going in a van."

"In a van!" It was a rare treat, and Sanjit gazed up in admiration. Suddenly, Uncle Vikram seemed like a hero again.

"You didn't think you'd be going all that way on foot, did you?" said Uncle Vikram, laughing. Soon, he went into an office to find someone while Sanjit waited outside. Sanjit wandered over to the white van, drew a face in the dust, and pondered what Uncle Vikram had just said. How far was "all that way"? He hadn't asked how far it was to the factory. He'd never thought about it.

Quickly, Sanjit rubbed away the face. If they caught him drawing in the dust they might be angry and not let him go to the carpet factory, and he'd have to go back with no job, no money, nothing to be proud of, and no ride in a van, either. When Uncle Vikram called his name, he jumped.

"Sanjit's even cleaning your van for you!" said Uncle Vikram to the short man beside him. "Make it sparkle, Sanjit!" He turned again to the short man. "He's a good worker."

The man, who said nothing to Sanjit, got into the van as Uncle Vikram walked around to the other side, pulled open the other door for Sanjit, and banged it shut after him. Then they were on their way, with Sanjit sitting stiffly alert and upright beside the driver as they rattled past little clusters of children in the street. He hoped they saw him. Soon they stopped to pick up two little girls, younger than Sanjit, who sat very close together behind him and giggled to each other.

The driver remained silent, and Sanjit felt too shy to speak to him. The little girls chattered to each other in low voices and eventually seemed to run out of things to say, but Sanjit was content to look out at the dry hills and bare landscape. Sometimes he saw a boy like himself leading animals to water, or fetching and carrying, or plowing. He had more than that to look forward to.

Sanjit was nibbling some of his chapati when they arrived in a town noisy with car horns, bicycle bells, animals being herded to market, and street traders engaged in frenzied bargaining. He tried to look in all directions at once. There were temples, and there were signs strung everywhere. Traders haggled in their stalls. The scene was overwhelming. Then the van turned down a quiet street, then another, and parked.

"Are we here?" asked Sanjit. There were buildings all around them, and he didn't know what a carpet factory looked like. "Is this the place?"

A busy street scene in the Indian city of Varanasi in Uttar Pradesh, similar to what Sanjit sees as he arrives in town

"You change here," said the man. It was all he had said the entire morning. "Out!"

Nobody had told Sanjit about any kind of change. His mother had given him a spare shirt to take with him. Did he mean that kind of change? There was nobody to ask except the silent, surly driver, and Sanjit didn't want to ask him. This felt wrong. The little girls looked at each other and managed a giggle, but it was a thin, nervous giggle.

"This way," said the driver. He gave Sanjit a swift push on the shoulder and led them down an alley into a yard where another, much bigger van waited. If they were simply changing vans, there was nothing to worry about, but Sanjit did worry. He was anxious. He hadn't expected this. They'd already taken a long journey, and this big van would take him even farther away from home.

Home. Home was a good place to be. He broke off a piece of the bread in his pocket and slipped it into his mouth. A big man with a pouting mouth appeared, glanced at the children, and took the driver aside.

Sanjit tried to make out what they were whispering about, but all he could hear were numbers – “Four hundred?” “Five hundred?” They were bargaining about something.

The big man glanced at Sanjit and the others and shook his head. “Three hundred each,” he said.

Sanjit was stunned. It was as if they were bargaining for... but no, they couldn’t be. You don’t buy children. The little girls were wide-eyed and silent.

“Get in the van!” the big man shouted suddenly, as he flung open the back doors. A waft of stifling heat swept over Sanjit with a stench of sweat and bodies. Three boys and two girls were already in there, sitting on the floor because there was nothing else to sit on. The driver brought them tea – nasty tasting, and not much of it – and stale bread. The doors slammed shut.

It was dark in there. Dark and hot. Then they were bumping and rattling away, and Sanjit had no idea where they might be going. He lost all track of time, but it seemed like hours. It must be night. He fell asleep, woke up, and slept again, and every time he woke up he felt a little colder, a little more terrified.

"It will be all right," he told himself. "It will be all right when we get to the carpet factory." He tried hard to believe this was true. He tried not to think of his family, and how every bump and every rattle was taking him farther away from them.

CHAPTER

4

The Looms

The van screeched, jolted, and forced Sanjit to wake up, but his eyelids were heavy and he longed to sleep again. Someone was yelling and dragging at him, and around him was a scrambling of feet as the other children awoke and got up. He stretched, rubbed his eyes, and stumbled into chaos and the cold night air.

He was greeted by the foul smell of the sewer, but then he was pushed into a room where bare light bulbs hung from the ceiling. It was a harsh, bright light, forcing him to squeeze his eyes shut against it.

Somebody was crying. When he peered through narrowed eyes he could see one of the little girls hugging the other as she wept quietly.

"You sleep here tonight," said a voice. Sanjit wasn't sure who was speaking. "You work in the morning." Faintly aware of sleeping children all around him, Sanjit curled up on a thin blanket and slept. He was hungry, thirsty, and cold, but more than that, he still needed to sleep.

"It will be all right in the morning when I start learning to make carpets," was the last thing he thought before he slept.

Sanjit woke up early to the sound of clanking and clattering. He sat bolt upright. He must be near the **carpet looms**! He was about to start learning.

Other children were stretching and yawning as they opened their eyes. When a man came into the room – a lean, bony man with big hands and feet and an ugly, scrawny mustache – they stopped talking at once.

There was something about the eyes of those children – something blank. When the big man snapped a few instructions, they scurried away like insects until only Sanjit and the other boys from the van were left. The little girls were gone. The man studied them coldly.

"You'll call me Mr. Sinu," he snapped. "This is my factory. You work for me. Whatever you want to know, you come and ask me. That way, you won't make mistakes and you'll stay out of trouble. If you can't find me, ask Mr. Nizam. You'll meet him this morning. Now, come and start learning."

"I'll learn quickly," thought Sanjit. "I want to be good at this." The noise of the looms grew louder as they followed Mr. Sinu to the closed door of the weaving room. His voice got louder too, but even so it was hard to hear what he said, especially if he turned his back to them. There was something about, "If you need the bathroom, if you absolutely have to go, it's that way, but you must ask permission first," and, "You're at the looms to work, not talk." Sanjit, straining to hear everything Mr. Sinu said, couldn't understand how anyone could have a conversation in that noise. Then the door to the weaving room was opened, and for the first time, Sanjit saw the towering looms.

They stretched from floor to ceiling, rows and rows of them, from one bare wall to the other. Long threads streamed like waterfalls from the floor to the ceiling, and at the bottom of each loom was the stretch of carpet the children were working on. Here, and stacked around the looms on sheets of plastic, were the amazing colored wools – green, red, violet, gold – like brilliant splashes of joy.

Sanjit looked up and around. The room was suffocatingly hot and stuffy with a putrid smell, but there were a couple of small windows open high up on the walls. Water ran down one wall. Where sunlight filtered in, he could see wispy wool fibers floating in the air.

At every loom was a bench, and at every bench sat a row of children. They had glanced up when Mr. Sinu brought in the newcomers, but now they continued their work, only raising their eyes for a second from time to time. It was long enough for Sanjit to clearly see their faces.

They were closed faces, like shut doors, locked boxes. When they looked down at their work they were tight with intense concentration. There was no room for mistakes in Mr. Sinu's factory.

"You sit here," said Mr. Sinu. "Now watch."

Sanjit sat down next to a small, very young boy. He could only be six or seven years old, and he was tying knots with quick fingers. Sanjit watched Mr. Sinu's big, bony hands twisting wool, tying knots, pressing them down with a tool like a small hammer,

pulling the wool tight, colors weaving in and out and through. It was gorgeous yarn, yellow and gold and thick.

"This yarn is made from the best wool," said Mr. Sinu. "We can't waste it, so make no mistakes. Sweep up any leftovers to use again." He looked up sharply. "Nizam!"

A man came to join them. He was like Mr. Sinu – Sanjit thought perhaps they were brothers – but shorter and broader.

"This is the new boy for this bench. What's your name, boy?"

"Sanjit," he called over the noise. The small boy at the loom coughed hoarsely.

"His name is Sanjit," said Mr. Sinu. "Watch him, Nizam, until he gets the idea." Then he scowled down at the coughing child. "Watch this one too. You know what he's like."

He stood up and glared down at the boy, who was swallowing hard in an attempt not to cough. "Mr. Nizam will be watching you, Bapi. Watch your step."

Bapi! That was the name of Sanjit's baby brother. Sanjit looked at the small boy again.

This time, Bapi couldn't help coughing, then hacking, out loud.

Sanjit got to work, twisting, tying, pushing, and pulling, watching the older boys at the bench to make sure he did everything correctly. Gold, blue, violet, green. He became hungry. His mouth became dry. Surely it must be time to eat by now? No. By the time I have done this next row, it will be time to eat. No. By the time I have finished this piece, it should be time to eat. No. His stomach ached with hunger and his throat burned by the time Mr. Nizam ordered them to leave the benches for a break.

Everyone seemed desperately thirsty. The first cup of water hardly made any difference to Sanjit, and he needed more. He could feel someone watching him as he drank. He looked up and saw Bapi.

"You get very thirsty in here," said Bapi. "It's the dust and the fluff in the air. It gets in your mouth. It makes you cough." There was a flare of mischief and a sudden bright smile. "It makes Mr. Sinu cranky."

It was the first time all day Sanjit had seen a child smile. Bapi had lively eyes.

There was plain rice to eat, but it couldn't compare to the rice Sanjit's mother made, and there wasn't much. Sanjit was surprised he finished it so quickly, and in no time the children had to return to the looms. The work went on, the deafening noise, the dusty air, the thirst, hour after hour until Sanjit thought it must be night, or the next day, and his fingers grew dry and shiny from handling the wool. Mr. Sinu would come to watch him and shake Bapi, who kept falling asleep. By the time the looms stopped, Sanjit felt as if he had been there forever. His eyes ached.

There was a meager amount of rice and tea before they slept. Sanjit ate with his back to the wall and his knees curled up. If he mastered the work quickly, perhaps he could move on and learn to do the really skilled work, hand-finishing the carpets. Then he would not have to go on doing the same thing over and over in the crashing racket and heat of the looms. It wouldn't always be like this.

Child laborers, similar to Sanjit and Bapi, sitting at their loom

He tried to think of the good things. There was Bapi, who was sitting beside him and falling asleep over the bowl he had scraped clean. There were those spellbinding colors, jewel bright and rich against the bare walls.

When he lay down to sleep, he still heard the looms clanking in his head, although he knew they had stopped. He thought longingly of his home.

He hid his face.

CHAPTER

Carpet Kids

Noise, dust, work. Noise, dust, work. That was all there was, all the next day, and the next, and the next. Noise, dust, work. Never enough food, never enough to drink, never enough sleep. It amazed Sanjit that he survived such agonizing fatigue and boredom,

and such hunger. His eyes throbbed from the close work in poor light and contaminated air. His fingers became sore. The dust made him cough. All the children coughed.

He kept his head down over his work and concentrated. He had seen Mr. Nizam beating children simply for working slowly, or talking at the looms, or making mistakes. Sanjit kept an eye on Bapi, who tended to fall asleep at his work. Sanjit was exhausted himself, and he was much older than Bapi. He had asked Bapi how old he was, and Bapi had smiled nervously and said, "I'm big now." He didn't seem to have any idea how old he was, but he couldn't be more than seven. Sanjit wondered how he wound up working there at all.

In the evenings, Bapi was asleep within five minutes of finishing his little bowl of rice. Sanjit would take the empty bowl from him and make him as comfortable as possible.

"You wouldn't think he was a real troublemaker, would you?" said an older boy one evening. Sanjit looked up in surprise.

"Vijay, you're teasing me," he said.

"It's the truth," said Manoj, Vijay's friend. The two boys seemed almost grown-up to Sanjit. Manoj squatted down on the floor beside him.

"On Bapi's first day here, he talked back to Mr. Sinu," he said. "He was beaten, then they locked him up. After they let him out, all he could think about was running away. He even tried it."

"What happened?" asked Sanjit.

"We found him trying to get out of a window and pulled him back," said Manoj.

"That was horrible!" exclaimed Sanjit. "Why would you do that to him?"

"Horrible?" said Manoj. "If we hadn't stopped him, they would have caught him. Then he would have gotten a *real* beating. He wouldn't have gotten far. They never do."

"If one kid ran and got away with it, we'd all run," said Vijay. "The bosses make sure we stay in."

"Wait a minute," said Sanjit, "we get out eventually, when we're old enough, right?"

Vijay shrugged. "Sure. They like kids to work here, not grown-ups. Kids have quick fingers and they move fast and don't argue too much. When you're too old to be worth keeping – when you're big enough to stand up for yourself – they give you the boot. Then you take care of yourself."

"Vijay and I, we'll be out of here soon," said Manoj. "We'll get work in a market or something."

"I don't understand..." began Sanjit. There was still something left of his dream, still a little faint hope. "You must both be real carpet weavers by now. You must have learned skilled work. They teach you that, don't they?"

Manoj and Vijay exchanged looks of pity. "Kid," said Manoj, "have you ever seen anything here except rows and rows of looms? No, and neither have we. All the finishing is done in locked rooms so we can't see and can't learn it. We're not here to learn the craft. We're carpet kids. We're here because we're cheap."

No training. No skills. No beautiful carpet for his mother. Sanjit's heart turned gray inside him.

"Do we get schooling?" he asked.

Manoj shook his head. "Never," he replied.

"What is our pay?"

"I got fifteen rupees last week," said Manoj. Fifteen rupees was almost nothing.

"I got seventy, all last year," said Vijay.

A few rupees now and then. He'd have to work for years even to earn enough money to get home.

Home. It was far away and impossible to get to. He must not think of it. He was a slave, and the only way out was to wait until he was too big to be useful anymore. He hoped Uncle Vikram didn't know what kind of a place he'd sent him to. He was sure his parents didn't, but he didn't know about Uncle Vikram.

Now, there was no one left to trust – except, of course, little Bapi. That was safer than trusting grown-ups. Bapi had a strong spirit. Slavery, hunger, and exhaustion had not taken the life out of his eyes. He didn't seem very smart, though, if he thought he could escape by running away.

"Take care of Bapi," thought Sanjit as he curled up on the floor. That would be something to live for.

CHAPTER

Bapi

Sanjit learned ways to cope with the unending days of work, tiredness, aching limbs, and sore fingers. He made up games to play inside his head while he worked. The one that kept his mind best occupied was choosing one color out of all the yarns.

Deep blue. How many things can I think of that are that shade of blue? The night sky. A butterfly wing. A bright jewel in a temple. Sometimes the water is that color. I haven't seen it look like that, but they say it does.

When Mr. Sinu comes around again, I'll pick a new color and give Bapi a little nudge to wake him up.

Orange. Orange for oranges, of course, and the inside of a ripe, cold mango. The thought of fresh, luscious mango made his mouth water, and he was happy for that. The dust made his mouth harsh and dry. Orange for lentils. What else, besides food? The sky at night. The robes of a holy man. Now change to rich, velvety purple. Bapi was nodding, falling asleep again.

"Bapi," he whispered. "Stay awake." Talking was dangerous. They'd be in trouble if Mr. Sinu caught them, but it would help Bapi to keep his eyes open. "Look at the purple on the loom. What does it make you think of?"

"My mom's scarf," said Bapi without a second's hesitation. He wriggled on the bench to shake himself more thoroughly awake. "She wears a scarf that color."

He stayed awake. Sanjit went on working. Purple, yellow, and orange again. Orange, like the sun as it was setting, big and furious. Perhaps the sun was furious because children worked for no pay in carpet factories. No pay, no play, no fun, no school – he jerked hard at the yarn.

Sanjit saw the swing of Mr. Sinu's arm and ducked, but the blow was not aimed at him. Bapi fell from the bench without a cry – there was just a despairing gasp as he hit the floor.

"Get up and get working," growled Mr. Sinu, "or I'll make sure you stay awake."

Sanjit burned to tell him that Bapi couldn't help it, that his body insisted on sleep, but he didn't dare. It would have created more hardship for everyone, including Bapi. He could only glare at Mr. Sinu's back as he walked away.

Orange for anger. Orange for fire. Bapi still lay on the floor, as if his little body was determined to take whatever rest it could. Sanjit slipped an arm around him and pulled him up.

"Keep going," he whispered. Bapi's skin felt hot and dry. His eyes were dull, and that was not like Bapi. Sanjit pulled him back on to the bench.

"Keep going," he said.

As the hours went on, Bapi's small, careful fingers began to tremble as they worked. He rubbed his eyes as if they hurt. Manoj came to sit at the other side of him so that he and Sanjit could correct his mistakes while sheltering him from the hateful eyes of Mr.

Sinu and Mr. Nizam. His head sagged heavily. He shivered. Bapi looked as if he couldn't even see the yarn, let alone wind it, and soon he had slumped helplessly against Sanjit. Bapi's skin was on fire.

"What is going on here?" Mr. Sinu demanded, striding toward them.

"He's sick, sir," said Sanjit. "He can't work."

Mr. Sinu shrugged. "Take him away," he said. "Leave him somewhere until he's shaken it off. Not in there," he added, as Manoj carried Bapi to the room where they slept. "I don't want you all catching something. Put him in a corner."

They laid him on sacks on the floor. Still shuddering, he curled up tightly, and they found a few rags to put over him.

"Who do you think you are, his mother and grandmother?" shouted Mr. Sinu. "You've got work to do."

Reluctantly, Sanjit left Bapi. He looked once over his shoulder as he turned back to the loom. The tall, white web reared up before him. All that yarn was for making carpets to sell, while Bapi lay with chattering teeth in a nest of rags.

There had to be a way out. Nothing so horribly unfair could be allowed to go on.

CHAPTER

Fever

Sanjit said exactly that to Vijay that night. They slept in the weaving shed so they could stay beside Bapi. “Nothing can be so horribly unfair and be allowed to go on.”

“It can,” said Vijay. “It’s been like this for years, and it’ll continue. You stop caring.”

"I won't," said Sanjit angrily.

There was still a little water in a cup, and he tilted it between Bapi's dry lips. Bapi hadn't eaten anything. He had hardly opened his eyes when they offered him food, but Sanjit knew it was crucial for him to drink. He was hot to the touch, but he shivered and hugged himself as if he were bitterly cold.

"There are the inspectors," said Vijay, "but I don't know if you can trust them."

"Who are the inspectors?" asked Sanjit.

"They come around to places like this, looking for kids working at the looms. Kids like Bapi, who are too little to work, and people like us, who work too long and don't get paid. Mr. Sinu watches for them, though. When there's an inspector coming, he forces all of us to hide in the storeroom. If the inspectors found us at the looms, they'd take us away immediately."

"Where would they take us?" asked Sanjit eagerly. It could be a little strand of hope. The inspectors might take him home! Vijay only shrugged.

"How do we know?" he asked. "I think they're supposed to take us somewhere safe, where we can go to school. Yet that's what we were told about coming here."

"I don't want to go home anyway," said Sanjit fiercely, willing himself to believe it. "I don't want to go home with no money and no present for my mother. I have to show I can accomplish something good before I see my family again."

Bapi's fever lasted for three long and terrifying days, and on the fourth he was still very weak. There was a heaviness in his eyes, as if he no longer cared about anything. He came back to sit at the bench beside Sanjit and Manoj, who tried to make it look as if he were working hard. In fact, he was still too exhausted and depleted to do anything. By the fourth night, he was back to sleeping in the big room with the other boys. He was asleep as soon as he left the loom, but he woke up when Sanjit lay down.

"Sanjit?" he said sadly. It was too dark to see his face, but Sanjit could imagine the large eyes staring at the ceiling. "Sanjit, do you ever think about your mother?"

"I try not to," said Sanjit.

"You must," said Bapi. "You must picture her face every night and every day, so you don't forget what she looks like. You have to remember, ready for when you see her again. I think of my mother all the time. She's very small. She has a purple scarf, like the deep purple yarn, and the most beautiful earrings anywhere in the world."

Sanjit smiled into the dark. It could be virtually anyone.

"Nobody else has earrings as nice as my mom's," continued Bapi. "They're long and gold, with thin dangly clusters like raindrops. She saves them for special days."

Sanjit could hear the smile in his voice. He must be getting better.

"What's her first name?" he asked. There was a long pause until Sanjit felt he shouldn't have asked.

"It was a long time ago," explained Bapi softly. "Her name was just Mom. She used to take me to see the goddess. It was just the two of us, and she would wear her earrings."

After that, Bapi recovered so quickly that Sanjit was astonished. He was restless and full of energy, as if he wanted to make up for the time he'd lost. Then, one morning, he wasn't there.

CHAPTER

8

Run

It wasn't long before Mr. Sinu, standing guard over the children as they walked to the looms, saw that Bapi was missing. There was some hushed, angry conversation between Mr. Sinu and Mr. Nizam. Soon, Mr. Nizam rushed off.

Sanjit knew they must be organizing a search. He didn't know what to do. The only option left was to hope as hard as he could.

A heavy hand grabbed Sanjit's shoulder, and he flinched. Mr. Sinu hauled him to his feet and banged him hard against the frame of the loom.

"You are his friend!" he barked. "What did he tell you?"

"Nothing," gasped Sanjit. He knew he must be brave, but his voice was thin with fear. Mr. Sinu jerked him by both shoulders, and Sanjit hit the wall with a force that knocked the breath out of him. His head throbbed and swam, and he felt as if he were going to be sick.

"Where is he?" demanded Mr. Sinu.

"I don't know." Sanjit forced out the words through the dizziness. Mr. Sinu could slam him again and Sanjit couldn't stop him, but Mr. Sinu didn't do it again. He let go so suddenly that Sanjit slumped to the floor.

Mr. Sinu began prowling between the looms, grabbing one child, then another, asking questions and, at last, giving up. Bapi would not have told anyone that he was running away, let alone which direction he would run.

Sanjit took his place at the loom, but his fingers tingled and shook as he worked. Purple yarn. Dark purple. Aubergine. A scarf for Bapi's mother. Bruises on a child's face. Mr. Sinu slapped him for being clumsy and sent him to sweep up the scraps on the floor.

With every minute, Bapi would be a little farther away. Sanjit pictured the bright, hopeful little face, the thin body, the small legs trotting on in determination. He was so small – Sanjit hoped he would get a ride on a cart or jump into the back of a wagon. Still, where would he go? Bapi couldn't remember where he came from.

Run, Bapi. Keep running.

More threads, more minutes, more hope. Then the door crashed open, and a child cried out with such misery and pain that it shivered in Sanjit's spine and twisted his heart. It could have been the voice of any desperate child bearing the unbearable, but Sanjit knew it was Bapi.

Bapi was bruised, bleeding, and filthy as Mr. Nizam dragged him through the door. Tear stains streaked the dust on his face. He put up one hand to protect his head as Mr. Nizam threw him to the floor, kicked him into a corner, and raised his fist.

Rage flared in Sanjit. All that mattered was to make this stop, now, immediately, to grab Mr. Nizam and twist, break, bite, anything, to make him stop pounding Bapi. Sanjit darted forward, but Manoj grabbed his arm.

"Don't do it!" whispered Manoj urgently. "You'll only make it worse!"

So instead, Sanjit stood shaking violently with clenched hands. Mr. Nizam dragged Bapi across the floor and pushed him against the frame of the loom as Mr. Sinu appeared with a piece of chain in his hands.

"This will keep him from running away," he said. He fastened the chain around Bapi's waist and around the loom, and locked it. He looked into Bapi's tearful eyes. "Now, if you want anything, Bapi – if you want a drink, or to go to the bathoom – well, that's your problem, isn't it?"

Mr. Nizam laughed, then stopped abruptly when he noticed the watching faces. "Does anyone else feel like running away? There's the door! Try it! If you don't want to try it, get to work. We don't feed you for nothing."

Sanjit tried to go on working. Bapi was curled up tightly with his head on his knees. Sanjit quickly laid a hand on his shoulder, but didn't dare do more than that in case Mr. Sinu or Mr. Nizam saw. He seized the yarn and jerked it angrily.

Sanjit felt what little hope he had left drain away. They were lost in a dense fog of injustice, cruelty, and anger. No one would ever find them.

When it was time to eat, Bapi was still **shackled** to the loom. There was no food for him. Sanjit shared his when the adults weren't looking, and some of the other children did the same. Bapi drank a little water, but he hardly ate anything. Sanjit thought it must hurt him to swallow.

Sooner or later this wretched day would be over. It would lead into another wretched day, but that might not be as vile as this one. Sanjit tried to plan ahead as he worked. How long would Bapi be left chained to the loom? All night? Probably. They wouldn't let him sleep in the big room with the others kids, who might actually be kind to him.

If Bapi had to stay there all night, so would Sanjit. He would have to hide when the

others were herded into the sleeping room and hope he wasn't noticed.

In a corner of the weaving room, rolls of finished carpets leaned against the wall. That would be the best place to hide, if he could wriggle in between them without being detected. Simply making his plans buoyed his spirits. It made him feel as if he were doing something for Bapi, and it took his mind off the groaning emptiness in his stomach.

Green yarn. Fresh grass. Leaves. Vegetables. Garlands. He was falling asleep. He jerked

himself up and tried to concentrate, but the long day was coming to an end. Bapi still sat in a tight ball, his head down, his arms around his knees. When the boys were sent to their sleeping room, Sanjit stayed with them until they had been counted, then watched for his opportunity.

Nobody was looking. He slipped away and wriggled in between the thick, heavy bolts of carpet.

He moved as fast as lightning, but there was a soft brushing noise as he eased the carpets aside. Fearfully, he looked up.

Vijay had seen him. Their eyes met. Vijay winked so swiftly that it hardly happened and then turned away.

"That's that," thought Sanjit. "Soon they'll be locked in for the night, Mr. Sinu and Mr. Nizam will go away, and I can go to Bapi. I just have to wait."

Yet there was something nobody had considered.

CHAPTER

Mr. Aghan

From his hiding place in the carpets, Sanjit heard an engine outside. There was nothing strange about that. Vans frequently arrived, delivering wool or yarn, or picking up carpets, but the sound of this engine was different somehow, unrecognizable.

Mr. Sinu went to the door. Then Sanjit heard the padding of hurried footsteps, urgent whispers between the two men, and a hoarse, hushed command from Mr. Nizam to the children.

"Get in there, stay there, and don't make a sound! Stay there, all of you, and don't move! Do you want the inspector to find you? He's a bad man! If he gets you, you're in big trouble! You'll wish you'd never been born!"

The key clicked briskly as Mr. Nizam locked the door. Then Sanjit heard him rush to the main doorway, where Mr. Sinu was talking to someone.

"Children?" Mr. Sinu was saying. "We only hire children over the age of fourteen. They work eight hours a day. Yes, they go to school after work, and we give them a half day each week for school too." He laughed loudly. "Of course we pay them! Oh, I'm sorry, you won't find any of them here now. They're local children, so they all go home at night."

The lies made Sanjit seethe with rage. He could dash out from his hiding place and shout. This was his opportunity! He could lead the inspector to the crowd of miserable, hungry children. Yet was the inspector really a compassionate person who only wanted the children to be taken care of, or would he cart them off to a slavery worse than this?

Sanjit was reluctant to trust the inspector. He had trusted his own uncle, once.

A creaking noise near him made him jump, gasp, and hold his breath. Somebody had just pushed open a door next to the sleeping room. That door was hardly ever used, and the hinges were stiff. Sanjit parted the carpets cautiously so he could see.

A man was walking down the weaving room, looking from left to right, bending down to inspect beneath the benches. He carried a flashlight and shone it into corners.

"That's smart," thought Sanjit. There must be two inspectors – one to keep Mr. Sinu and Mr. Nizam talking while the other could sneak in through the back way.

The flashlight beam fell on the one figure forgotten by everyone except Sanjit: Bapi.

Sanjit looked from Bapi to the man and back. Now, as never before, his place was to protect Bapi. He watched, listened, and waited. If the inspector was friendly to Bapi, everything was okay. If he harmed him, Sanjit could jump from his hiding place and – well, he wasn't sure what he would do, but he wouldn't let anyone harm Bapi.

He stood still and taut as a wire. The hair on his arms prickled with cold and terror. The inspector knelt beside Bapi, and Sanjit saw his face.

It was a kind face. A gentle hand stroked Bapi's curly hair, and when Bapi flinched, the man spoke softly.

"I won't hurt you. Will you tell me your name? Will you let me help you?"

Bapi's head stayed down.

"I'll tell you who I am," said the man. "I'm Mr. Aghan. I'm very handsome. I have green striped skin and wiggly ears and a pink nose that I wear upside down."

Sanjit smiled. He watched to see if Bapi would turn his head and look, which was clearly what Mr. Aghan wanted him to do. Bapi didn't move a muscle.

"I'll tell you what I do," Mr. Aghan said gently. "I help children who don't like working in carpet factories. Children like you."

He glanced past Bapi at the closed door, and Sanjit could see he was apprehensive. He didn't know how long it might be before Mr. Sinu or Mr. Nizam came in and discovered them, or how long it would take to release Bapi from his chains. The key was probably in Mr. Sinu's office.

Sanjit looked again at Mr. Aghan's face. Nobody at the factory ever looked at a child like that, with care and concern. He parted the carpets and stepped forward.

"His name is Bapi," he said. "He's my friend." Then, realizing in a rush that if he were going to trust this man, he must trust him completely, he blurted out, "They chained him up for running away. There are more of us, but the rest of them are in the sleeping room."

Sanjit knelt down and placed his hands gently on Bapi's shoulders. "Bapi," he said, "this man can help you."

There was no response. Sanjit turned to Mr. Aghan.

"I think I could find the keys in Mr. Sinu's office, sir," he said.

"Do that," said Mr. Aghan with another nervous glance at the door. Then he gave a smile of encouragement that reached Sanjit's heart. "What's your name?"

"Sanjit," he answered. Then he turned and darted away to the office.

It wasn't difficult to find the keys. The inspectors had arrived too suddenly for the bosses to put anything out of sight. He took them, then froze.

Mr. Sinu was coming to the office.

"You can examine the books," he was saying to the inspector. "I keep a record of all the payments to the children. Don't you believe me? Don't you believe that we pay them for their excellent work?"

They were at the office door. Sanjit hid behind the filing cabinet and made himself as small as he could. Mr. Sinu's voice suddenly became quiet and friendly.

"Please remind me," he was saying. "What is the fee for an inspection?"

"There is no fee," said the inspector sternly.

"Call it expenses, then," said Mr. Sinu. "Three hundred? Four?"

The last time Sanjit had heard a conversation like this, he was being crammed into a van with the other unsuspecting children. They had been sold and bought. Now, Mr. Sinu wanted to pay the inspector to forget about them. He shrank further behind the filing cabinet. Then, from somewhere in the looms, came the firm voice of Mr. Aghan.

"In addition to buying children as slave labor, you are trying to bribe an inspector," he said. "Do you think any rich customers will buy your carpets when they hear about this?"

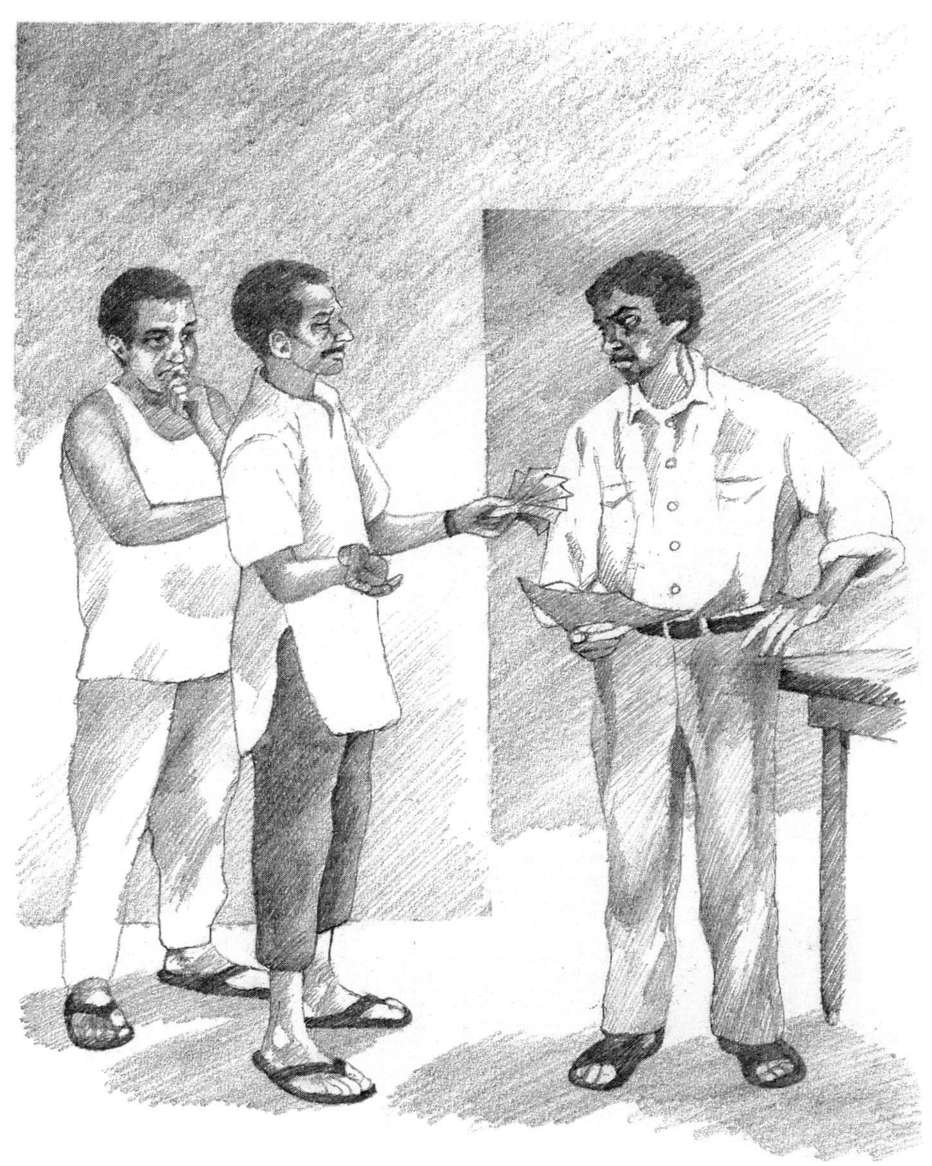

Mr. Sinu and Mr. Nizam began to argue, lying, complaining, and making excuses. It gave Sanjit the chance he needed. He slipped out with the keys and opened the door of the sleeping room.

"It's safe to come out," he said. Then he crossed the room in front of the infuriated faces of Mr. Sinu and Mr. Nizam and unlocked Bapi's chains.

Bapi turned at last to Mr. Aghan. His eyes were still pink with tears.

"Can you find my mom?" he said.

CHAPTER

10

Hopes

Sanjit woke up in the morning feeling as if he were in paradise. He had forgotten what it was like to wake up feeling this way, happy and looking forward to the day.

The night before, the children from the factory had been taken in a van to a long

building in the city. It seemed full of children already, but there was room enough for a few more clean mattresses on the floor, and there had been supper! Not just rice, but lentils and vegetables too, and enough to eat without feeling as hungry as you were when

you started. Bapi's cuts and bruises had been examined and cleaned by a doctor who was sympathetic and gentle, reminding Sanjit of his grandmother. Her name was Dr. Mumtaz.

Lying awake at night, Sanjit talked to the older boys in the room and found his highest hopes had been met. Everything here really was as good as it looked. This was a place for children who were taken from any employers who mistreated them, not just carpet factories.

This time, there would be education. This time, there would be enough of everything. Bapi, who had fallen asleep almost as soon as he was fed, was wide awake now, lying on his side on the mattress next to Sanjit and watching with deep, dark eyes.

"Are you all right?" asked Sanjit.

"Do we get more to eat?" asked Bapi.

They did, after they'd all washed and dressed, and later that morning Mr. Aghan called Sanjit into his office. Sunshine poured in through a window.

"Tell me about yourself," said Mr. Aghan.

Sanjit told him everything about why he had left home, and how Uncle Vikram had arranged for him to go to the carpet factory. "I don't think he understood what it was like," he said, "or surely he wouldn't have sent me there."

Mr. Aghan did not comment on what Uncle Vikram might or might not have known. "Do you want to go home?" he asked.

Home.

The very word conjured up a picture of his mother making garlands. He squeezed his eyes shut tightly and opened them again.

"Yes," Sanjit said, but at home he had wanted to get away. "I do, but I have to earn money. I need to learn a skill. I want to learn to read and write. I want to do something that matters."

Mr. Aghan nodded. "We can arrange that here, if your parents agree. First, you'll receive schooling. By the time you've got some education under your belt, we'll know what you're best at and arrange training for you. We'll make sure you go to a place where you'll be taught well. You'll have decent food, reasonable hours, and no beatings. You'll be treated with respect. Does that sound good?"

"Yes, sir!" answered Sanjit happily.

"We'll have to find out what your parents think," said Mr. Aghan, "but, after everything you've told us, it shouldn't be difficult to find them." He leaned across the desk and folded his hands. "We're having more trouble with your little friend. He doesn't remember much about where he's from."

"He knows a little about his mother," said Sanjit. "She has..."

"Yes, the purple scarf, the long gold earrings, and she's small," said Mr. Aghan, smiling warmly. "It doesn't help much, does it? He must have been very young when he was sold."

Under the desk, Sanjit saw Mr. Aghan's toes curl in his sandals. "The very idea of selling children is poisonous, Sanjit," he said. "I don't know if we'll ever find Bapi's mother. We'll do what we can, though. Get him to talk to you. He might remember something important."

Sanjit's lessons started the next day, and the pattern of squiggles and swirls on the classroom board convinced him that he'd never learn to read and write. However, day by day, it was easier. He learned to tell one letter

from another, to get them facing the right way, and to put together words and sentences. He learned about numbers and shapes, and he loved the patterns they made. He learned to calculate and to use drawing tools.

Bapi discovered books. He was not yet learning to read, but he would sit contentedly on the floor and look at the pictures. He was doing that one afternoon while Sanjit was drawing shapes with a ruler.

"We'll make a **draftsperson** out of you yet," said Mr. Aghan, who was watching. Dr. Mumtaz was with him.

"We'll make an **engineer** out of him," she said. "You have real talent, Sanjit."

"I want to bring money home to my mother," said Sanjit. "I wanted to make her a gift. I had hoped I could weave her a carpet."

"That's her!" a small voice chirped eagerly from the floor.

Everyone looked down. Bapi had his finger on the open page of his book. He turned his face up to see if Sanjit was watching.

"That's the goddess," he said. "My mother used to take me there!"

Sanjit, Mr. Aghan, and Dr. Mumtaz all knelt on the floor around Bapi and his book. "My mom took me there," he explained, pointing to a jeweled figure in a shrine. "She used to go to the goddess about her bad hand." He frowned in concentration. "She had a bad hand. She hurt it, and it got all crumpled." He curled his fingers. "See? just like that."

Sanjit could feel the beam of triumph on Mr. Aghan's face before he saw it. "Now we're getting somewhere!" he said.

"I know where that is," said Dr. Mumtaz, bending over the book, "and we're looking for a woman with a paralyzed hand. That narrows it down a little. Bapi, why didn't you tell us about her hand?"

Bapi lowered his head. "It didn't seem like a nice thing to tell about someone," he whispered.

Sanjit didn't tell Bapi, but he thought the paralyzed hand could explain a lot. There wasn't much work for anyone who had lost the use of one hand. No wonder she had to part with her son. She probably thought he'd be safe and taken care of.

Before long, there was something else for Sanjit to think about. In addition to his lessons, he was sent once a week to help a carpenter. He learned to work with the grain of the wood, and which woods were hard and which were soft, and how to use a saw, a hammer, and a plane. The carpenter let him use scraps of wood for himself, and he was making a little dish for his mother. He sanded it and stained it so it was as smooth as pure silk and gleamed like oil.

She would come. One day, she would come. When Sanjit was finished, he polished the bowl every day so it wouldn't have a single speck of dust on it when she saw it.

❖

Some of the children from the carpet factory had left. Training positions had been found for Manoj and Vijay. Parents came for a few, but not all. Sanjit discovered again the fun of kicking a soccer ball around in the warm, welcoming sunshine. Bapi discovered pencils and paper. At first nobody could tell what he had drawn because he covered all his pictures with heavy scribbles, but in time he started to draw a woman. A purple woman. He couldn't add her earrings, he said, because he didn't have gold.

Sanjit never knew why he felt different on one particular day, but he did. He felt as if something new, something promising, was in the air. He couldn't concentrate in the carpenter's shop and was relieved when it was time to go home. The other boys were going to play soccer before supper, but Sanjit didn't want to.

"I want to," said Bapi, and Sanjit still felt responsible for Bapi. He went reluctantly, following the other boys as they ran ahead, hoping they'd be back soon. Then a van rocked and rattled to a stop in front of them. Sanjit knew. His heart was rising with joy even before the first glimpse of his mother, and he raced to meet her, wrapping himself around the flowing smoothness of her best sari, her warmth, her familiar smell – then he looked past her.

Dr. Mumtaz was helping another woman down from the van. Sanjit saw her purple scarf and her long earrings. He saw the hand with the curled fingers. He looked around for Bapi – and Bapi stood staring, wide-eyed and open-mouthed, as if all the bliss in the world had filled him, and he would burst.

Story Background

Beautiful carpets are made in many parts of the world, particularly in Middle Eastern and Asian countries. The ones pictured here are from northern India.

Typical rugs from Srinigar, a town in the northern state of Kashmir, India

However, carpet weaving is not the only industry that uses child slaves; nor is it only in India that child labor occurs.

There are children forced to make hundreds of cigarettes each day, to clean the homes of wealthy families, to toil farming the land – and all for no pay, and often accompanied by severe beatings and other horrific abuses.

These children in Pakistan are forced to turn bricks over as they cool. They are used because they are small and light and therefore won't break the bricks.

Indian children, who were once child slaves, carry signs to show their defiance of this practice.

Children have started to organize in order to demand better protection in the form of **legislation** and controls. Like Sanjit in this story, they are concerned that their livelihoods should not be affected because they *need* to earn money for their families. They simply want decent and humane working conditions, access to education, and fair pay.

There are many organizations working to abolish child slavery. *New Internationalist* **(www.newint.org)** is an online magazine that has reported extensively on this issue. To learn more about child labor and exploitation and what you can do to help, you can visit **www.freethechildren.org**.

Finally, if you are buying a carpet or rug from overseas, check to see that it carries the RUGMARK (**www.rugmark.org**) or similar guarantee of nonslave manufacture.

Indian carpets for sale in England

Index

Glossary

carpet loom – a large upright loom used for weaving carpets

chapati – an unleavened bread that is a staple food in some parts of India

dhal – a lentil dish often cooked with spices

draftsperson – someone who has been trained to draw sketches or plans of things, including buildings and machines

engineer – someone who plans and designs things such as bridges and buildings

legislation – the process of changing or creating laws

sari – a length of cloth draped around the body; worn by some Indian women

shackle – to bind with chains or other means in order to keep someone captive